**James Triplett**

# Surviving Introduction to Finance

**Surviving Introduction to Finance**

Other books by James Triplett
*On Organizational Effectiveness and Change: The Graduate Years and Beyond, Volume II*
*On ethics, diversity, and conflict: The graduate years and beyond, Volume I*
*On leadership, salad, and the American Revolution*
*Organizational Design: A holistic view*

# Surviving Introduction to Finance

**James Triplett**

Nouveau Erudit
2014

First Printing: 2014

ISBN 978-1-312-18298-1

Nouveau Erudit
3804 Raspberry Street

Erie, PA 16509-1322

www.askthatprofessor com

# Dedication

As always, to my wife Michelle.  Without you I would not be ...

# Contents

# Surviving Introduction to Finance

# Acknowledgements

My thanks to Dr. Neal Shambaugh, IDT Program Coordinator at West Virginia University, for his guidance on the structure of this book as part of my design project, a workshop that has the same name as this book.

# Surviving Introduction to Finance

# Introduction

The idea behind this book came from my experiences teaching and tutoring finance students. I found over the years some common items that were the source of learner frustration with learning the concepts in this course. I observed my courses and tutoring sessions for a few semesters and grouped the common areas of learner reported concerns and results of formative and summative feedback into five categories which form the five chapters in this book.

Each chapter stands alone or the book may be approached from the beginning through the last chapter. One objective of this book was to organize and write it in a manner that it can serve as a useful handbook for the learner to be reviewed and referenced, as needed. And, as a means to assist the learner, I have provided some of the templates and others at my website www.askthatprofessor.com for free download and use.

Surviving Introduction to Finance

# Chapter I: Algebra review

One of the obstacles I have noted with learners first entering an introduction to finance course is it may have been some time since one completed an algebra class or the scheduling of the finance course is placed before a math class. The latter can sometimes happen when a course prerequisite does not list a math class. Many of the formulas one finds in the introduction to finance course are basic algebra and there are instances where a learner may be required to manipulate a given equation a number of ways to solve for each unknown variable. Other instances involving combining like terms or using the Distributive Property. Finally, as it may have been some time since an algebra class, order of operations may be an issue. Typically, when order of operations is the problem, learners express anxiety as they set up the formula correctly and still get an incorrect answer when matched against the examples in a book, an answer key, or an online course supplement. We begin our review with order of operations.

## Order of operations

As expressions and equations may have parentheses, exponents, and other math operations, there exists a means to consistently simplify them. Think of order of operations as directions for simplifying expressions and equations you will find in finance. The specific order ensures you consistently simply these as you work to solve for a variable. You may recall the use of the acronym PEMDAS to help with the order:

1) Parentheses
2) Exponents
3) Multiplication and division, from left to right
4) Addition and subtraction, from left to right

## Surviving Introduction to Finance

First, look for parentheses, then exponents, followed by multiplication and division. Then, move to addition and subtraction, left to right. Consider this brief example to illustrate:

11-5-2=?

As there are no parentheses, exponents, multiplication and division, move to addition and subtraction, from left to right. First is 11-5 = 6. Put 6 back into the equation in the place of 11-5 to get 6-2=? Finally, simplify 6-2 to get 4. Thus, 11-5-2=4.

How about another example?  5 + 12/3 = ?

First step is division (recall a fraction is nothing more than division). 12 divided by 3 is 4. Replace 4 where 12/3 was and reevaluate. 5 + 4 = ? All that is left is addition. 5+4 = 9.

Consider this example: 4 / (2+6). Parentheses are first, so do the math inside them. (2+6) = 8. Replace (2+6) with 8 and reevaluate. 4/8 is division (or simply a fraction). Thus, 4/8 is 1/2, or, if you prefer 0.50. Two decimal places are the preferred minimum in most finance courses.

Now, consider this one:

$3+3^2/14-2$

Treat the numerator and denominator as if they have ( ) around them. The small 2 above the second 3 is an exponent. This means to you multiply the base number, 3, by itself the number of times in the exponent. 3 squared is 3 * 3 or 9. Replace the 3 squared with 9. Now, we have (3+9) / (14-2). Do the math inside the ( ) to get 12 / 12. Now, all that is left is division, with 12 divided by 12 equal to 1.

Next up is another example, shown with each iteration:

$6*4^3-(8+2)$

$6*4^3-(10)$

$6*(4*4*4)-10$

$6*64-10$

$384-10$

$374$

Here, the parentheses are first, exponent next, then multiplication followed by subtraction.

The following are some tips for completing aspects of order of operations. Calculators have an exponent key. Enter coefficient first, then   key, then exponent. For example, consider

$4^5$

Enter 4 on a calculator, then look for a key similar to this:

$y^x$

then press 5.  Press = key or Enter to get 1,024.

For Excel (can also use Calc from Open Office or a Google spreadsheet), math operations are completed by first typing in the = sign to tell Excel what follows is a math operation.  The ^ key (Shift+6) is the exponent key.  Using the same example above, type in:

=4^5

then Enter.  The result is 1,024.

An additional note to keep in mind is most calculators also include ( ) keys for grouping so entire problems may be entered. Excel allows for the same use of ( ), but do not use [ ] or { }.  Excel has built in order of operations for many problems.  If you want to

**Surviving Introduction to Finance**

ensure Excel does certain calculations first, add your own groupings with ( ). Consider: 4+3/8+2. In Excel type in:

=(4+3)/(8+2)

which produces 0.70, while:

=4+3/8+2

produces 0.6375 because Excel does 3/8 first. So, if one 's problem resembles the former example, use ( ) to group the problem.

So, whether you manage order of operations by hand, by calculator or by a spreadsheet, keep in mind PEMDAS and, remember, double-check your work, just to be certain.

## Combining like terms

We next turn our attention to combining like terms, an essential concept one finds while following order of operations. Monomials are numbers, variables (letters or symbols that represent a value), or a product (result of multiplication) of numbers and variables raised to a power (exponent). Examples of these include:

-2

8x

$y^5$

$24x^3y^8, -ab^2c^5$

Terms that have the same variable and are raised to the same power can be combined. Consider 9y-y. This expression can be combined because both variables are the same. There is an implied number next to the single y, which is 1, or 9y-1y. Perform subtraction of 9-1 and place next to y factor to produce 8y.  The following may also be combined because both variables are the same as are the exponents:

$$-a^2 + 5a^2$$
$$-1 + 5 = 4$$
$$4a^2$$

You will note here that the coefficients (the numbers that are products of a squared) are -1 and 5.  Combine these to get a 4, then place the a squared next to it (recall, this means 4 times a squared).

Here is another example:

$$3y^3 + y^2 - y$$

While the variables are the same, the exponents are not so these cannot be combined.

Variables may also be symbols, as one may find in some finance courses.  Beta, β, is used in the Capital Asset Pricing Model (CAPM) to find the expected return of a security:

$$E(r) = R_{RF} + \beta(R_M - R_{RF})$$

Beta is a number that is either provided in finance problems or derived (typically it is given in introductory finance courses).  Here is an example that uses order of operations and combining like terms using the CAPM:

$$If \_ R_{RF} \_ is \_ 0.03; \beta \_ is \_ 1.2; and \_ R_M \_ is \_ 0.07$$
$$E(r) = 0.03 + 1.2(0.07 - 0.03)$$
$$0.03 + 1.2(0.04)$$
$$0.03 + 0.048$$
$$0.078$$
$$7.8\%$$

The risk-free rate is 0.03, beta is 1.2 and the return on the market is 0.07.  Insert these where you see the symbols, follow order of operations, and arrive at 0.078. To convert this to a % format, multiply by 100 (and to move from % to a decimal equivalent, divide by 100).

In sum, when it comes to combining like terms, focus on the variables and the exponents to see if they can be combined. Sometimes, you will end up with an expression or equation that cannot be combined or simplified.

# Distributive property

Distributive property is important in finance as many finance problems require one to simplify equations with grouped values, like the previous CAPM example. The basic idea is for real numbers a, b, and c, a(b+c) = ab + ac and a(b-c) = ab-ac. What this means is each number on the outside multiplied by each number on the inside. Pay attention to the sign for each. For example:

3(x+2)

3(x+2) or 3 times x *and* 3 times +2

This produces 3x + 6. Remember, each item on the inside times the item on the outside.

Next, how about 14-(3-x)? For this one, it can be rewritten as 14-1(3-x) as the 1 is implied. Thus, following order of operations and applying distributive property:

-1(3-x) produces -1 times 3 and -1 times –x

14-3+x (remember, minus times a minus = +). Because only 14 and -3 can be combined, the result is 11+x.

To summarize the Distributive Property, focus on multiplying what is outside the parentheses times each item (and remember the sign) inside the parentheses.

## Solving for a variable

Formulas are a large part of finance. Typically, one will be presented a standard formula with all but one unknown and you will have to find the unknown. This involves manipulating the equation. The steps involved are: 1) Use distributive property to clear parenthesis; 2) Get all terms containing the variable on one side of the equal side; 3) Isolate variable by multiplication, division, addition, and or subtraction.

Consider this example: 8x-18=2-2x.

First, move -18 to the right side by adding the opposite of -18:

$8x - 18 + 18 = 2 - 2x + 18$.

Adding 18 to both sides clears it from the left and moves it to the right without changing the nature of the equation. This produces:

8x=20-2x

Next, add 2x to each side:

8x+2x=20-2x+2x

10x =20

Then, divide both sides by 10 as division is the opposite of 10 times x:

10x/10=20/10

**Surviving Introduction to Finance**

The 10's cancel out leaving x on the left: 20/10=2.

x=2

A common formula in finance is the Dividend Discount Model (DDM):

$$P_0 = D_1/(r-g)$$

This says the price today of a stock is equal to the expected dividend one period from now divided by the difference of the required return and the growth rate. Example: what is the price of a stock that is expected to pay a dividend of $2.00, has a required return of 12%, and a growth rate of 6%? (note, enter % values as decimal equivalents):

$$P_0 = 2/(0.12-0.06)$$
$$P_0 = 2/0.06 = \$33.33$$

Many times, one may have to solve for a different variable than price as three other variables are given. For example, solve for r:

$$P_0 = D_1/(r-g)$$
$$P_0(r-g) = D_1$$
$$(r-g) = D_1/P_0$$
$$r-g+g = (D_1/P_0)+g$$
$$r = (D_1/P_0)+g$$

To rearrange this, multiply both sides by (r-g). Then, divide both sides by Po. Add g to both sides. Then, can input the values for D1, Po, and g to solve for r.

Another common finance problem is a future value problem:

$$FV = PV(1+r)^t$$

If PV is $100, r is 6%, and t is 5 years, then:

$$FV = 100(1+0.06)^5$$
$$FV = 100(1.06)^5$$
$$FV = 100(1.3382)$$
$$FV = \$133.82$$

How about a present value problem?

$$PV = FV/(1+r)^t$$

If I have $500 that will be paid in 5 years and the current rate of return is 10%, then:

$$PV = 500/(1+0.10)^5$$
$$PV = 500/(1.10)^5$$
$$PV = 500/1.61$$
$$PV = \$310.56$$

In sum, you will note how solving for a variable includes order of operations and combining like terms as well as the possibility of the Distributive Property. So, like following order of operations, take a moment before working with each equation to determine the steps you should follow.

# Surviving Introduction to Finance

# Chapter II – Time value of money (TVM)

The basic idea behind the concept of time value of money is $1 received today is worth more than $1 in the future. Or, in other words, $1 received in the future is worth less than $1 today. This is because interest can be earned on the money. The connecting piece or link between present (today) and future is the interest rate.

There are four types of Time Value of Money (TVM) formulas: 1) Present value of a lump sum, 2) Present value of an annuity, 3) Future value of a lump sum, and 4) Future value of an annuity. In the process of determining which approach to use, there are two questions one may ask (such as when working on TVM homework problems). The first question is are you looking to find a value in the future or the present? In other words, do you have a value today that you want to know the value of tomorrow; or, do you have a value in the future that you want to know the value of today? The second question is are you dealing with a single amount or a series of equal cash flows per period (typically a year - and the emphasis must be on the word equal as unequal cash flows are not an annuity)?

An additional thought on the annuity is important before continuing on. An annuity is a stream or series of equal payments to be received in the future. The payments are assumed to be received at the end of each period (ordinary). Any payments that are paid at the beginning of the period are referred to as an annuity due. A good example of an annuity is a lottery, where the winner is paid over a number of years.

## Future value

Let us begin with the future value and examine how to approach this using the TVM table approach as well as formula. Recall, the Future Value (FV) is what money today will be worth at some point in the future. The single cash flow - or lump sum - table approach uses FV = PV x FV(IF) where FV(IF) is the future value interest factor in one of the four TVM tables typically used with this approach. and looks something like this:

| FUTURE VALUE INTEREST FACTOR - FVIF (ONE CASH FLOW) | | | | | | | | | | | |
|---|---|---|---|---|---|---|---|---|---|---|---|
| **Number of Periods** | | | | | | | | **Interest Rate** | | | |
| 1% | 2% | 3% | 4% | 5% | 6% | 7% | 8% | 9% | 10% | 11% | 12% |
| 1.010 | 1.020 | 1.030 | 1.040 | 1.050 | 1.060 | 1.070 | 1.080 | 1.090 | 1.100 | 1.110 | 1.120 |
| 1.020 | 1.040 | 1.061 | 1.082 | 1.103 | 1.124 | 1.145 | 1.166 | 1.188 | 1.210 | 1.232 | 1.254 |
| 1.030 | 1.061 | 1.093 | 1.125 | 1.158 | 1.191 | 1.225 | 1.260 | 1.295 | 1.331 | 1.368 | 1.405 |
| 1.041 | 1.082 | 1.126 | 1.170 | 1.216 | 1.262 | 1.311 | 1.360 | 1.412 | 1.464 | 1.518 | 1.574 |
| 1.051 | 1.104 | 1.159 | 1.217 | 1.276 | 1.338 | 1.403 | 1.469 | 1.539 | 1.611 | 1.685 | 1.762 |
| 1.062 | 1.126 | 1.194 | 1.265 | 1.340 | 1.419 | 1.501 | 1.587 | 1.677 | 1.772 | 1.870 | 1.974 |
| 1.072 | 1.149 | 1.230 | 1.316 | 1.407 | 1.504 | 1.606 | 1.714 | 1.828 | 1.949 | 2.076 | 2.211 |
| 1.083 | 1.172 | 1.267 | 1.369 | 1.477 | 1.594 | 1.718 | 1.851 | 1.993 | 2.144 | 2.305 | 2.476 |
| 1.094 | 1.195 | 1.305 | 1.423 | 1.551 | 1.689 | 1.838 | 1.999 | 2.172 | 2.358 | 2.558 | 2.773 |
| 1.105 | 1.219 | 1.344 | 1.480 | 1.629 | 1.791 | 1.967 | 2.159 | 2.367 | 2.594 | 2.839 | 3.106 |
| 1.116 | 1.243 | 1.384 | 1.539 | 1.710 | 1.898 | 2.105 | 2.332 | 2.580 | 2.853 | 3.152 | 3.479 |
| 1.127 | 1.268 | 1.426 | 1.601 | 1.796 | 2.012 | 2.252 | 2.518 | 2.813 | 3.138 | 3.498 | 3.896 |

The formula approach is:

$$FV = PV(1+r)^t$$

The variable r is the interest rate and the exponent t number of periods. You may also find t interchanged with n and i interchanged with r for the rate. These are the same formula, just different variables. Focus on the formula mechanics rather than the differences in variables.

An example will help. Suppose you have $10,000 invested for 10 years at 8%. Using FV = PV * FV(IF), it is FV = 10,000 * 2.159. This 2.159 is found in the FV(IF) table by cross-referencing 8% and 10 periods, as noted here:

**FUTURE VALUE INTEREST FACTOR - FVIF (ONE CASH FLOW)**

| Number of Periods | 1% | 2% | 3% | 4% | 5% | 6% | 7% | 8% | 9% | Interest Rate 10% | 11% |
|---|---|---|---|---|---|---|---|---|---|---|---|
| 1 | 0 | 1.020 | 1.030 | 1.040 | 1.050 | 1.060 | 1.070 | 1.080 | 1.090 | 1.100 | 1.110 |
| 2 | 0 | 1.040 | 1.061 | 1.082 | 1.103 | 1.124 | 1.145 | 1.166 | 1.188 | 1.210 | 1.232 |
| 3 | 0 | 1.061 | 1.093 | 1.125 | 1.158 | 1.191 | 1.225 | 1.260 | 1.295 | 1.331 | 1.368 |
| 4 | 1 | 1.082 | 1.126 | 1.170 | 1.216 | 1.262 | 1.311 | 1.360 | 1.412 | 1.464 | 1.518 |
| 5 | 1 | 1.104 | 1.159 | 1.217 | 1.276 | 1.338 | 1.403 | 1.469 | 1.539 | 1.611 | 1.685 |
| 6 | 2 | 1.126 | 1.194 | 1.265 | 1.340 | 1.419 | 1.501 | 1.587 | 1.677 | 1.772 | 1.870 |
| 7 | 2 | 1.149 | 1.230 | 1.316 | 1.407 | 1.504 | 1.606 | 1.714 | 1.828 | 1.949 | 2.076 |
| 8 | 3 | 1.172 | 1.267 | 1.369 | 1.477 | 1.594 | 1.718 | 1.851 | 1.993 | 2.144 | 2.305 |
| 9 | 4 | 1.195 | 1.305 | 1.423 | 1.551 | 1.689 | 1.838 | 1.999 | 2.172 | 2.358 | 2.558 |
| 10 | 1.10 | | | | | | 67 | 2.159 | 2.367 | 2.594 | 2.839 |
| 11 | 1.11 | | | | | | 105 | 2.332 | 2.580 | 2.853 | 3.152 |
| 12 | 1.127 | 1.268 | 1.426 | 1.601 | 1.796 | 2.012 | 2.252 | 2.518 | 2.813 | 3.138 | 3.498 |
| 13 | 1.138 | 1.294 | 1.469 | 1.665 | 1.886 | 2.133 | 2.410 | 2.720 | 3.066 | 3.452 | 3.883 |

It is also the value one finds with the $(1+r)^t$ portion of the formula $FV = PV * (1+r)^t$. $(1+0.08)$ raised to the power of 10 is 2.159. Thus, the future value using these approaches is \$21,598.25.

If you like Excel, you can use its FV function. I recommend building a small table in Excel and then saving this so you can use it as a FV calculator. The inputs for the FV function are RATE, NPER, PMT and PV. RATE is the interest rate, NPER the number of periods, PMT any annuity, and PV the present value. TYPE is the selection for timing type; enter a 0 for a first payment that begins at the end of the first period and 1 for a payment that begins immediately (or at the beginning). If you omit this, the default is 0. The specific function in Excel is:

=FV(RATE,NPER,PMT,PV,TYPE)

where the value itself is entered where you see the inputs. Remember, enter interest rate in Excel as a decimal format instead of % format. And, recall from Chapter 1 that cash outflows are entered as negative values so PV is entered as a negative value. Another way of looking at this is you write a check to a bank for a deposit that will then grow and be returned to you (as a positive cash flow) at maturity. Here is how I set up Excel for something like this, then I use cell references in the formula so I can reuse this over and over (by saving it). In the adjacent cell to Future value and assuming this is created starting in cell A1, =FV(B4/B6,B5*B6,B3,-B2,0). More on the compounding periods shortly.

| Future value | |
|---|---|
| Present value | $ 10,000.00 |
| Payment | $ - |
| Rate | 8.00% |
| Time | 10 |
| Compound. Per. | 1 |
| Future value | $21,589.25 |

When you are dealing with multiple identical cash flows, the TVM table approach uses FV(A) = A x FV(IFA) where FV(IFA) is the future value interest factor for annuity. The formula looks like this:

$$FV_A = A\,(1+i)^{n-1} + A\,(1+i)^{n-2} + \dots A\,(1+i)^1 + A\,(1+i)^0$$

$$FV_A = A\left(\frac{(1+i)^n - 1}{i}\right)$$

Expressed another way, FV = A * (((1+i)^n)-1)/i). Here, A is the equal cash flow, i is used for interest rate (remember, it can also be r), and n for time (remember, it can also be t). This formula means the future value of an annuity is the sum of all compounded cash flows each year to the future. The FV(IFA) table looks like this:

| Number of Periods | FUTURE VALUE INTEREST FACTOR FOR ANNUITY - FVIFA (MULTIPLE, IDENTICAL CASH FLOW) | | | | | | | | Interest Rate | | | |
|---|---|---|---|---|---|---|---|---|---|---|---|---|
| | 1% | 2% | 3% | 4% | 5% | 6% | 7% | 8% | 9% | 10% | 11% | 12% |
| 1 | 1.000 | 1.000 | 1.000 | 1.000 | 1.000 | 1.000 | 1.000 | 1.000 | 1.000 | 1.000 | 1.000 | 1.000 |
| 2 | 2.010 | 2.020 | 2.030 | 2.040 | 2.050 | 2.060 | 2.070 | 2.080 | 2.090 | 2.100 | 2.110 | 2.120 |
| 3 | 3.030 | 3.060 | 3.091 | 3.122 | 3.153 | 3.184 | 3.215 | 3.246 | 3.278 | 3.310 | 3.342 | 3.374 |
| 4 | 4.060 | 4.122 | 4.184 | 4.246 | 4.310 | 4.375 | 4.440 | 4.506 | 4.573 | 4.641 | 4.710 | 4.779 |
| 5 | 5.101 | 5.204 | 5.309 | 5.416 | 5.526 | 5.637 | 5.751 | 5.867 | 5.985 | 6.105 | 6.228 | 6.353 |
| 6 | 6.152 | 6.308 | 6.468 | 6.633 | 6.802 | 6.975 | 7.153 | 7.336 | 7.523 | 7.716 | 7.913 | 8.115 |
| 7 | 7.214 | 7.434 | 7.662 | 7.898 | 8.142 | 8.394 | 8.654 | 8.923 | 9.200 | 9.487 | 9.783 | 10.089 |
| 8 | 8.286 | 8.583 | 8.892 | 9.214 | 9.549 | 9.897 | 10.260 | 10.637 | 11.028 | 11.436 | 11.859 | 12.300 |
| 9 | 9.369 | 9.755 | 10.159 | 10.583 | 11.027 | 11.491 | 11.978 | 12.488 | 13.021 | 13.579 | 14.164 | 14.776 |
| 10 | 10.462 | 10.950 | 11.464 | 12.006 | 12.578 | 13.181 | 13.816 | 14.487 | 15.193 | 15.937 | 16.722 | 17.549 |
| 11 | 11.567 | 12.169 | 12.808 | 13.486 | 14.207 | 14.972 | 15.784 | 16.645 | 17.560 | 18.531 | 19.561 | 20.655 |
| 12 | 12.683 | 13.412 | 14.192 | 15.026 | 15.917 | 16.870 | 17.888 | 18.977 | 20.141 | 21.384 | 22.713 | 24.133 |

Let us look at an example. Suppose you invest $1,000 at the end of each year for four years at 10%. How much will you have at the end of four years? Using FV(A) = A x FV(IFA), it is FV = 1,000

* 4.641. This 4.641 is found in the FV(IFA) table by cross-referencing 10% and 4 periods, as noted here:

FUTURE VALUE INTEREST FACTOR FOR ANNUITY - FVIFA (MULTIPLE, IDENTICAL CAS

| Number of Periods | | | | | | Interest Rate | | | | | |
|---|---|---|---|---|---|---|---|---|---|---|---|
| | 1% | 2% | 3% | 4% | 5% | 6% | 7% | 8% | 9% | 10% | 11% |
| 1 | 00 | 1.000 | 1.000 | 1.000 | 1.000 | 1.000 | 1.000 | 1.000 | 1.000 | 1.000 | 1.000 |
| 2 | 10 | 2.020 | 2.030 | 2.040 | 2.050 | 2.060 | 2.070 | 2.080 | 2.090 | 2.100 | 2.110 |
| 3 | 30 | 3.060 | 3.091 | 3.122 | 3.153 | 3.184 | 3.215 | 3.246 | 3.278 | 3.310 | 3.342 |
| 4 | 60 | | | | | | | | 573 | 4.641 | 4.710 |
| 5 | 5.101 | 5.204 | 5.309 | 5.416 | 5.526 | 5.637 | 5.751 | 5.867 | 5.985 | 6.105 | 6.228 |
| 6 | 6.152 | 6.308 | 6.468 | 6.633 | 6.802 | 6.975 | 7.153 | 7.336 | 7.523 | 7.716 | 7.913 |

The use of the formula $FV = A * ((((1+i)^n)-1)/i)$ looks like this:

$FV = 1000 * ((((1+.10)^4)-1)/0.10)$

Remember order of operations covered in Chapter 1. And, using the Excel approach listed above - in fact, the exact same approach just with values entered in different cells - produces this:

| Future value | |
|---|---|
| Present value | $ - |
| Payment | $ 1,000.00 |
| Rate | 10.00% |
| Time | 4 |
| Compound. Per. | 1 |
| Future value | ($4,641.00) |

Notice here, the present value cell is not filled in because in this example, one does not begin with a balance on hand. The payment is the annuity amount. Notice, as well, that when the payment is listed as a positive, the future value is negative. Had the payment been entered as a negative, the future value would be positive, but the same absolute value. This is a reminder that one person's cash out is the other side's cash in. For example, if a bank receives $1,000 from you as a deposit, it is a cash inflow the bank and a cash outflow to you. At maturity, it is a cash outflow to the bank as it returns the money to you and a cash inflow to you.

If the same scenario exists but payment begins immediately, use FV Annuity Due formula: $FV = A(1+i)*((((1+i)^t)-1)/i)$, or

**Surviving Introduction to Finance**

FV(IFA) table value times A * (1+i) or 4,641 * (1000 * (1+0.10) = 5,105.10. The formula looks like this:

$$FV = 1000*(1+0.10)*((((1+0.10)^4)-1)/0.10) = \$5,106.10$$

And the Excel looks like this (I added another cell below to show the difference between timing types 0 and 1:

| Future value | | |
|---|---|---|
| Present value | $ | - |
| Payment | $ | 1,000.00 |
| Rate | | 10.00% |
| Time | | 4 |
| Compound. Per. | | 1 |
| Future value | | ($4,641.00) |
| Future value, annuity due | | ($5,105.10) |

The only difference in these formulas is I replaced a 0 for TYPE with a 1. When set up this way, you can see the difference beginning a payment immediately and making the first one at the end of a period. You may see problems like this in your homework so this set up can be quite useful.

## Present value

Now, we turn our attention to present value. Present Value (PV) is what money at some point in the future is worth today. The single cash flow - or lump sum - table approach uses PV = FV x PV(IF) where PV(IF) is the present value interest factor, an example of which is:

| PRESENT VALUE INTEREST FACTOR - PVIF (ONE CASH FLOW) | | | | | | | | | | | |
|---|---|---|---|---|---|---|---|---|---|---|---|
| **Number of Periods** | | | | | | | | | **Interest Rate** | | |
| 1% | 2% | 3% | 4% | 5% | 6% | 7% | 8% | 9% | 10% | 11% | 12% |
| 0.990 | 0.980 | 0.971 | 0.962 | 0.952 | 0.943 | 0.935 | 0.926 | 0.917 | 0.909 | 0.901 | 0.893 |
| 0.980 | 0.961 | 0.943 | 0.925 | 0.907 | 0.890 | 0.873 | 0.857 | 0.842 | 0.826 | 0.812 | 0.797 |
| 0.971 | 0.942 | 0.915 | 0.889 | 0.864 | 0.840 | 0.816 | 0.794 | 0.772 | 0.751 | 0.731 | 0.712 |
| 0.961 | 0.924 | 0.888 | 0.855 | 0.823 | 0.792 | 0.763 | 0.735 | 0.708 | 0.683 | 0.659 | 0.636 |
| 0.951 | 0.906 | 0.863 | 0.822 | 0.784 | 0.747 | 0.713 | 0.681 | 0.650 | 0.621 | 0.593 | 0.567 |
| 0.942 | 0.888 | 0.837 | 0.790 | 0.746 | 0.705 | 0.666 | 0.630 | 0.596 | 0.564 | 0.535 | 0.507 |
| 0.933 | 0.871 | 0.813 | 0.760 | 0.711 | 0.665 | 0.623 | 0.583 | 0.547 | 0.513 | 0.482 | 0.452 |
| 0.923 | 0.853 | 0.789 | 0.731 | 0.677 | 0.627 | 0.582 | 0.540 | 0.502 | 0.467 | 0.434 | 0.404 |
| 0.914 | 0.837 | 0.766 | 0.703 | 0.645 | 0.592 | 0.544 | 0.500 | 0.460 | 0.424 | 0.391 | 0.361 |
| 0.905 | 0.820 | 0.744 | 0.676 | 0.614 | 0.558 | 0.508 | 0.463 | 0.422 | 0.386 | 0.352 | 0.322 |
| 0.896 | 0.804 | 0.722 | 0.650 | 0.585 | 0.527 | 0.475 | 0.429 | 0.388 | 0.350 | 0.317 | 0.287 |
| 0.887 | 0.788 | 0.701 | 0.625 | 0.557 | 0.497 | 0.444 | 0.397 | 0.356 | 0.319 | 0.286 | 0.257 |

(Rows correspond to Number of Periods 1 through 12.)

The formula approach is:

$$PV = FV\left(\frac{1}{(1+i)^n}\right)$$

An example will help. Suppose you are to receive $1,464 in four years. If you were to sell that future receipt to someone today how much would you get if the discount rate is 10% per year? Using PV = FV * PV(IF) the interest factor is 0.683, as found in this table:

| PRESENT VALUE INTEREST FACTOR - PVIF (ONE CASH FLOW) | | | | | | | | | | |
|---|---|---|---|---|---|---|---|---|---|---|
| **Number of Periods** | | | | | | | | | **Interest Rate** | |
| 1% | 2% | 3% | 4% | 5% | 6% | 7% | 8% | 9% | 10% | 11% |
| 0. | 0.980 | 0.971 | 0.962 | 0.952 | 0.943 | 0.935 | 0.926 | 0.917 | 0.909 | 0.901 |
| 0. | 0.961 | 0.943 | 0.925 | 0.907 | 0.890 | 0.873 | 0.857 | 0.842 | 0.826 | 0.812 |
| | .942 | 0.915 | 0.889 | 0.864 | 0.840 | 0.816 | 0.794 | .772 | 0.751 | 0.731 |
| 0.9 | 0.924 | | | | | | | 08 | 0.683 | 0.659 |
| 0.951 | 0.906 | 0.863 | 0.822 | 0.784 | 0.747 | 0.713 | 0.681 | 0.650 | 0.621 | 0.593 |

PV = $1,464 x 0.683, which is $1,000. This is just the FV example above in reverse to demonstrate the utility of each approach. An Excel template can be set up, just like with FV:

## Surviving Introduction to Finance

| Present value | | |
|---|---|---|
| Future value | $ | 1,464.00 |
| Payment | $ | - |
| Rate | | 10.00% |
| Time | | 4 |
| Compound. Per. | | 1 |
| Present value | | $999.93 |

The set up is the same and the function: =PV(RATE,NPER,PMT,FV,TYPE). Notice how the only difference here is PV and FV have switched places in the function.

The future value of an annuity TVM table formula is: PV(A) = A x PV(IFA), where PV(IFA) is the future value interest factor for annuity. The table looks like this:

| Number of Periods | PRESENT VALUE INTEREST FACTOR FOR ANNUITY - PVIFA (MULTIPLE, IDENTICAL CA | | | | | | | | Interest Rate | | | |
|---|---|---|---|---|---|---|---|---|---|---|---|---|
| | 1% | 2% | 3% | 4% | 5% | 6% | 7% | 8% | 9% | 10% | 11% | 12% |
| 1 | 0.990 | 0.980 | 0.971 | 0.962 | 0.952 | 0.943 | 0.935 | 0.926 | 0.917 | 0.909 | 0.901 | 0.893 |
| 2 | 1.970 | 1.942 | 1.913 | 1.886 | 1.859 | 1.833 | 1.808 | 1.783 | 1.759 | 1.736 | 1.713 | 1.690 |
| 3 | 2.941 | 2.884 | 2.829 | 2.775 | 2.723 | 2.673 | 2.624 | 2.577 | 2.531 | 2.487 | 2.444 | 2.402 |
| 4 | 3.902 | 3.808 | 3.717 | 3.630 | 3.546 | 3.465 | 3.387 | 3.312 | 3.240 | 3.170 | 3.102 | 3.037 |
| 5 | 4.853 | 4.713 | 4.580 | 4.452 | 4.329 | 4.212 | 4.100 | 3.993 | 3.890 | 3.791 | 3.696 | 3.605 |
| 6 | 5.795 | 5.601 | 5.417 | 5.242 | 5.076 | 4.917 | 4.767 | 4.623 | 4.486 | 4.355 | 4.231 | 4.111 |
| 7 | 6.728 | 6.472 | 6.230 | 6.002 | 5.786 | 5.582 | 5.389 | 5.206 | 5.033 | 4.868 | 4.712 | 4.564 |
| 8 | 7.652 | 7.325 | 7.020 | 6.733 | 6.463 | 6.210 | 5.971 | 5.747 | 5.535 | 5.335 | 5.146 | 4.968 |
| 9 | 8.566 | 8.162 | 7.786 | 7.435 | 7.108 | 6.802 | 6.515 | 6.247 | 5.995 | 5.759 | 5.537 | 5.328 |
| 10 | 9.471 | 8.983 | 8.530 | 8.111 | 7.722 | 7.360 | 7.024 | 6.710 | 6.418 | 6.145 | 5.889 | 5.650 |
| 11 | 10.368 | 9.787 | 9.253 | 8.760 | 8.306 | 7.887 | 7.499 | 7.139 | 6.805 | 6.495 | 6.207 | 5.938 |
| 12 | 11.255 | 10.575 | 9.954 | 9.385 | 8.863 | 8.384 | 7.943 | 7.536 | 7.161 | 6.814 | 6.492 | 6.194 |

The formula is:

$$PV_A = A\left(\frac{1}{(1+i)}\right)^1 + A\left(\frac{1}{(1+i)}\right)^2 + ...A\left(\frac{1}{(1+i)}\right)^n$$

$$PV_A = A\left(\frac{1-\left(\frac{1}{(1+i)^n}\right)}{i}\right)$$

Another variation is: PV = A * ((1-(1/((1+i)^n)))/i). An example will help illustrate, as we covered above. Suppose your uncle is going to give you $1,000 per year for four years at the end of each year. You need to inform your accountant what the value of that is today (assume 10% return). The TVM formula is PV = $1,000 x 3.170 where the table value is found by:

| Number of Periods | 1% | 2% | 3% | 4% | 5% | 6% | 7% | 8% | 9% | 10% | 11% |
|---|---|---|---|---|---|---|---|---|---|---|---|
PRESENT VALUE INTEREST FACTOR FOR ANNUITY - PVIFA (MULTIPLE, IDENTIC — Interest Rate

| 1 | .990 | 0.980 | 0.971 | 0.962 | 0.952 | 0.943 | 0.935 | 0.926 | 0.917 | 0.909 | 0.901 |
| 2 | .970 | 1.942 | 1.913 | 1.886 | 1.859 | 1.833 | 1.808 | 1.783 | 1.759 | 1.736 | 1.713 |
| 3 | | | | | | | | | 2.531 | 2.487 | 2.444 |
| 4 | .902 | | | | | | | | .240 | 3.170 | 3.102 |
| 5 | 4.853 | 4.713 | 4.580 | 4.452 | 4.329 | 4.212 | 4.100 | 3.993 | 3.890 | 3.791 | 3.696 |
| 6 | 5.795 | 5.601 | 5.417 | 5.242 | 5.076 | 4.917 | 4.767 | 4.623 | 4.486 | 4.355 | 4.231 |

The formula is PV =1000*((1-(1/((1+0.1)^4)))/0.1), which equals $3,1770. An Excel template set up in the previous FV example can be used:

| Present value | |
|---|---|
| Future value | $ - |
| Payment | $ 1,000.00 |
| Rate | 10.00% |
| Time | 4 |
| Compound. Per. | 1 |
| Present value | ($3,169.87) |

If the same scenario exists but payment begins immediately, use PV Annuity Due formula: A + A*((1-(1/(1+i)^(n-1)))/i) or =1000+1000*((1-(1/(1+0.1)^(4-1)))/0.1) = $3,486.85. For table, use 3 years, 10% * A or 2.487 * 1,000 = $3,487.00. Adding a section below the present value in Excel, like what was done for future value, looks like this:

| Present value | |
|---|---|
| Future value | $ - |
| Payment | $ 1,000.00 |
| Rate | 10.00% |
| Time | 4 |
| Compound. Per. | 1 |
| Present value | ($3,169.87) |
| Present value, annuity due | ($3,486.85) |

# Adjusting for Non-Annual Compounding

Interest is often compounded quarterly, monthly, or semiannually in the real world.  Since the time value of money tables assume annual compounding, an adjustment must be made as follows:

1)    the number of years is multiplied by the number of compounding periods;  and
2)    the annual interest rate is divided by the number of compounding periods

An example will illustrate.  Suppose you have $10,000 invested for 10 years at 8%, with semiannual compounding. Semiannual is 2 times per year.  The time, n, is multiplied by 2 (10*2 = 20) and the rate, i, is divided by 2 (0.08 / 2 = 0.04).  Using the FV lump sum TVM table, FV = $10,000 X 2.191:

FUTURE VALUE INTEREST FAC

| Number of Periods | 1% | 2% | 3% | 4% | 5% |
|---|---|---|---|---|---|
| 1 | 1.010 | 1.020 | 1.030 | 1.040 | 1.050 |
| 2 | | 1.040 | 1.061 | 1.082 | 1.103 |
| 3 | | 1.061 | 1.093 | 1.125 | 1.158 |
| 4 | | 1.082 | 1.126 | 1.170 | 1.216 |
| 5 | | 1.104 | 1.159 | 1.217 | 1.276 |
| 6 | | 1.126 | 1.194 | 1.265 | 1.340 |
| 7 | | 1.149 | 1.230 | 1.316 | 1.407 |
| 8 | | 1.172 | 1.267 | 1.369 | 1.477 |
| 9 | | 1.195 | 1.305 | 1.423 | 1.551 |
| 10 | | 1.219 | 1.344 | 1.480 | 1.629 |
| 11 | | 1.243 | 1.384 | 1.539 | 1.710 |
| 12 | | 1.268 | 1.426 | 1.601 | 1.796 |
| 13 | | 1.294 | 1.469 | 1.665 | 1.886 |
| 14 | | 1.319 | 1.513 | 1.732 | 1.980 |
| 15 | | 1.346 | 1.558 | 1.801 | 2.079 |
| 16 | | 1.373 | 1.605 | 1.873 | 2.183 |
| 17 | | 1.400 | 1.653 | 1.948 | 2.292 |
| 18 | | 1.428 | 1.702 | 2.026 | 2.407 |
| 19 | | 1.457 | 1.754 | 2.107 | 2.527 |
| 20 | 1.220 | | 1.806 | 2.191 | 2.653 |
| 21 | 1.232 | 1.516 | 1.860 | 2.279 | 2.786 |
| 22 | 1.245 | 1.546 | 1.916 | 2.370 | 2.925 |

and the formula FV = 10,000 * $(1+0.04)^{20}$ = $21,911.23.  Returning to the Excel template created earlier, just enter 2 for compounding periods:

| Future value | |
|---|---|
| Present value | $ 10,000.00 |
| Payment | $ - |
| Rate | 8.00% |
| Time | 10 |
| Compound. Per. | 2 |
| Future value | $21,911.23 |

You will likely find you prefer a certain approach as you gain practice with these. Unless you are specifically directed by your instructor to demonstrate proficiency in one approach, choose the one with which you are most comfortable.

## Compound problem – bond valuation

A bond is a compound time value of money problem as the typical bond contains a lump sum (par value returned at maturity) and a series of periodic payments. After a bond has been issued and begins trading in the secondary market, the market rates are used to price the bond while the stated coupon rate on the bond is used to determine the periodic payments. Excel is the ideal utility for bond valuation problems as one may find rate (also known as yield to maturity) and current price, among others, when given key information.

Consider a bond with a stated coupon rate of 8% and 15 years left to maturity that is currently selling at a discount to par at $923.05. What is the yield to maturity? Use Excel's =RATE function:

=RATE(NPER,PMT,PV,FV,TYPE)

Notice how the same input terms are present, just rearranged. NPER = 15; pmt is found by taking the 8% coupon times the par value (assumed to be $1,000 unless otherwise informed) so 0.08*1000 = 80; PV = -923.05 (remember to enter as a negative value), and fv = 1000 (the par value). Type = 0.

**Surviving Introduction to Finance**
=RATE(15,80,-923.05,1000,0) = 0.0895 or 8.95%

Note, if Excel returns 9%, just expand the format 2 decimal places. And, please recall the negative / positive inputs for cash inflows and outflows.

Now, consider a bond with a stated coupon rate of 10% and 8 years left to maturity. New bonds of this risk level are currently paying 9%. What is current price? Use Excel's =PV function:

=PV(RATE,NPER,PMT,FV,TYPE)

Rate is the current market rate of 9%, or 0.09; nper is 8; pmt is the coupon rate times par, or 10% * 1000 = 100; fv is the par value of 1000 (assumed to be 1000 unless otherwise informed), and type is 0.

=PV(0.09,8,100,1000,0) = $1,055.35

This bond is selling at a premium to par as its stated coupon rate is higher than what the new ones of comparable risk are selling for in the current market.

A financial calculator may be used for these type of problems as well. The same approach taken for Excel to get the inputs is exactly the same. The only difference is that one enters each value given on a financial calculator by typing in each value followed by the appropriate calculator key (i.e. N for time, I/Y for rate, PV for present value, FV for future value, and PMT for coupon payment).

Templates for time value of money may be found at my website:

www.askthatprofessor.com

# Chapter III - Accounting statement / ratios / capital structure review

We next turn our attention to the accounting statements one works with in an introduction to finance. It is likely, but not always assured, you will have had an accounting course before finance as most programs require some exposure to introduction to finance; however, each school has discretion in its program design as to whether or not this is the case. As such, this chapter serves as a review if it has been some time since your introduction to accounting or it is sufficient to introduce you to the accounting concepts you will be exposed to in an introduction to finance course.

There are four financial statements one may encounter, but only two of them are the primary focus of the introduction to finance course, the balance sheet and the income statement, and will be the focus of this chapter. The other two financial statements are the statement of cash flows and the statement of retained earnings. Ratio analysis incorporates the financial statement information to make comparisons over time or across the organization's industry.

## Balance sheet

A balance sheet is a point in time statement that shows what a company owns – its assets – and how it paid for them – its liabilities (debt / obligations) and equity (owner investment / interest in company), or L&E (L for liabilities and E for equity). Think of it this way: In a simple company that begins with an owner investment of $100 cash, the balance sheet will look like this:

Assets
  Cash          $100
  Total assets  $100

L&E

**Surviving Introduction to Finance**

| | |
|---|---|
| Liabilities | $0 |
| Equity | $100 |
| Total L&E | $100 |

Now, if the owner borrows $1,000 to buy a car, then the balance sheet will look like this:

Assets
| | |
|---|---|
| Cash | $100 |
| Car | $1,000 |
| Total assets | $1,100 |

L&E
| | |
|---|---|
| Loan | $1,000 |
| Liabilities | $1,000 |
| Equity | $100 |
| Total L&E | $1,100 |

The company owns $100 cash and a $1,000 car paid for with $1,000 in debt and $100 in owner contributions. Over time, with more assets and ways to pay for them, the balance sheet becomes more detailed, as noted here:

| Assets | 2013 Amount | Percent | 2012 Amount | Percent |
|---|---|---|---|---|
| *Current assets* | | | | |
| Cash | $ 2,250.00 | 6.85% | $ 1,945.00 | 5.58% |
| Acc. Rec. | $ 4,510.00 | 13.74% | $ 3,187.00 | 9.14% |
| Inventory | $ 16,820.00 | 51.23% | $ 18,796.00 | 53.89% |
| *Total current assets* | $ 23,580.00 | 71.82% | $ 23,928.00 | 68.60% |
| | | | | |
| *Plant and Equipment* | | | | |
| Equipment | $ 14,250.00 | 43.41% | $ 13,450.00 | 38.56% |
| Accumulated Depreciation | $ (5,000.00) | | $ (2,500.00) | |
| *Total P&E* | $ 9,250.00 | 28.18% | $ 10,950.00 | 31.40% |
| | | | | |
| Total Asset | $ 32,830.00 | 100.00% | $ 34,878.00 | 100.00% |
| | | | | |
| **Liabilities** | | | | |
| *Current liabilities* | | | | |
| Acc. Payables | $ 1,650.00 | 5.03% | $ 2,218.00 | 6.36% |
| Wages Payables | $ 479.00 | 1.46% | $ 594.00 | 1.70% |
| *Total current liabilities* | $ 2,129.00 | 6.48% | $ 2,812.00 | 8.06% |
| | | | | |
| *Long-term liabilities* | | | | |
| Note payable | $ 13,212.00 | 40.24% | $ 12,225.00 | 35.05% |
| *Total long-term liab.* | $ 13,212.00 | 40.24% | $ 12,225.00 | 35.05% |
| | | | | |
| Total liabilities | $ 15,341.00 | 46.73% | $ 15,037.00 | 43.11% |
| | | | | |
| **Owner's Equity** | | | | |
| Capital (equity) | $ 17,489.00 | 53.27% | $ 19,841.00 | 56.89% |
| | | | | |
| Total liabilities & Equity | $ 32,830.00 | 100.00% | $ 34,878.00 | 100.00% |

As the balance sheet grows over time, there may be more subcategories added. An additional means to organize the balance sheet is current and non-current items. Current assets are those items on the asset side that are reasonably expected to be converted to cash – or are cash – within 1 year. These include items like cash, marketable securities, accounts receivable, and inventory. Current liabilities are those items on the liability side that are expected to be paid within 1 year. These include items like accounts payable, wages payable, and any portion of long-term debt that has less than one year left to pay off.

Balance sheets can be analyzed up / down at a given point in time (vertical) as well as over time (horizontal):

# Surviving Introduction to Finance

| Assets | Amount (2013) | Percent (2013) | Amount (2012) | Percent (2012) | Increase / decrease Amount | % change |
|---|---|---|---|---|---|---|
| Current assets | | | | | | |
| Cash | $ 2,250.00 | 6.85% | $ 1,945.00 | 5.58% | $ 305.00 | 15.68% |
| Acc. Rec. | $ 4,510.00 | 13.74% | $ 3,187.00 | 9.14% | $ 1,323.00 | 41.51% |
| Inventory | $ 16,820.00 | 51.23% | $ 18,796.00 | 53.89% | $ (1,976.00) | -10.51% |
| Total current assets | $ 23,580.00 | 71.82% | $ 23,928.00 | 68.60% | $ (348.00) | -1.45% |
| | | | | | | |
| Plant and Equipment | | | | | | |
| Equipment | $ 14,250.00 | 43.41% | $ 13,450.00 | 38.56% | | |
| Accum. Depreciation | $ (5,000.00) | | $ (2,500.00) | | | |
| Total P&E | $ 9,250.00 | 28.18% | $ 10,950.00 | 31.40% | $ (1,700.00) | -15.53% |
| | | | | | | |
| Total Asset | $ 32,830.00 | 100.00% | $ 34,878.00 | 100.00% | $ (2,048.00) | -5.87% |
| | | | | | | |
| Liabilities | | | | | | |
| | | | | | | |
| Current liabilities | | | | | | |
| Acc. Payables | $ 1,650.00 | 5.03% | $ 2,218.00 | 6.36% | $ (568.00) | -25.61% |
| Wages Payables | $ 479.00 | 1.46% | $ 594.00 | 1.70% | $ (115.00) | -19.36% |
| Total current liabilities | $ 2,129.00 | 6.48% | $ 2,812.00 | 8.06% | $ (683.00) | -24.29% |
| | | | | | | |
| Long-term liabilities | | | | | | |
| Note payable | $ 13,212.00 | 40.24% | $ 12,225.00 | 35.05% | | |
| Total long-term liab. | $ 13,212.00 | 40.24% | $ 12,225.00 | 35.05% | $ 987.00 | 8.07% |
| | | | | | | |
| Total liabilities | $ 15,341.00 | 46.73% | $ 15,037.00 | 43.11% | $ 304.00 | 2.02% |
| | | | | | | |
| Owner's Equity | | | | | | |
| Capital (equity) | $ 17,489.00 | 53.27% | $ 19,841.00 | 56.89% | $ (2,352.00) | -11.85% |
| | | | | | | |
| Total liabilities & Equity | $ 32,830.00 | 100.00% | $ 34,878.00 | 100.00% | $ (2,048.00) | -5.87% |

Vertical analysis shows how each item on the asset / L&E side is a percent of the total. This can show how composition changes over time. For example, cash was 5.58% of assets in 2012 but increased to 6.85%. This can happen for a variety of reasons; over time, this may signal such things as tighter credit terms, better management of inventory, or perceptions of increasing risk that lead managers to hold more cash.

|  | 2012 | | |
| --- | --- | --- | --- |
| Assets | Amount | | Percent |
| *Current assets* | | | |
| Cash | $ 1,945.00 | | 5.58% |
| Acc. Rec. | $ 3,187.00 | | 9.14% |
| Inventory | $ 18,796.00 | | 53.89% |
| Total current assets | $ 23,928.00 | | 68.60% |
| | | | |
| *Plant and Equipment* | | | |
| Equipment | $ 13,450.00 | | 38.56% |
| Accumulated Depreciation | $ (2,500.00) | | |
| Total P&E | $ 10,950.00 | | 31.40% |
| | | | |
| Total Asset | $ 34,878.00 | | 100.00% |

|  | 2013 | | |
| --- | --- | --- | --- |
| Assets | Amount | | Percent |
| *Current assets* | | | |
| Cash | $ 2,250.00 | | 6.85% |
| Acc. Rec. | $ 4,510.00 | | 13.74% |
| Inventory | $ 16,820.00 | | 51.23% |
| Total current assets | $ 23,580.00 | | 71.82% |
| | | | |
| *Plant and Equipment* | | | |
| Equipment | $ 14,250.00 | | 43.41% |
| Accumulated Depreciation | $ (5,000.00) | | |
| Total P&E | $ 9,250.00 | | 28.18% |
| | | | |
| Total Asset | $ 32,830.00 | | 100.00% |

Now, how about an example? Recall, a balance sheet is set up in the following format:

Asset = Liabilities + Equity

Each side of the balance sheet is ordered by first listing current items followed by long-term items. Current assets are those items on the asset side that are reasonably expected to be converted to cash – or are cash – within 1 year. Current liabilities are those items on the liability side that are expected to be paid within 1 year. The balance

**Surviving Introduction to Finance**

sheet must balance; that is, the assets must equal the combined total of the liabilities and equity. This is always a good thing to check for when putting together a balance sheet.

Assemble a balance sheet with the following information:

Cash – 4500; Inventory 21,980; Accounts payable – 11,500; Wages Payable – 1,400; Acc. Depreciation – 3,000; Note payable – 21,900; Capital (equity) – 17,380; Accounts receivable – 6200; Equipment – 22,500.

First, sort the items into one of three categories:

Assets include: Cash – 4500; Inventory 21,980; Accounts receivable – 6200; Acc. Depreciation – 3,000; and Equipment 22,500

Liabilities include: Accounts payable – 11,500; Wages Payable – 1,400; Note payable – 21,900

Equity has just one item: Capital (equity) – 17,380

Next, sort the items into current and non-current:

Current assets include: Cash – 4500; Inventory 21,980; Accounts receivable – 6200

Non-current assets include: Acc. Depreciation – 3,000; and Equipment 22,500

Current Liabilities include: Accounts payable – 11,500; Wages Payable – 1,400

Non-current liabilities: Note payable – 21,900

Equity has just one item: Capital (equity) – 17,380

Now list in order of liquidity (ease of converting to cash):
Cash                                 4500

| Inventory | 21,980 | |
| Accounts receivable | 6200 | |
| Current Assets: | | 32,680 |
| Equipment | 22,500 | |
| Acc. Depreciation | 3,000 | |
| Net Equipment | | 19,500 |
| Total assets | | 52,180 |

Now, the L&E side:

| Wages Payable | 1,400 | |
| Accounts payable | 11,500 | |
| Total current liab. | | 12,900 |
| Note payable | | 21,900 |
| Total liabilities | | 34,800 |
| | | |
| Capital (equity) | | 17,380 |
| | | |
| Total liabilities and equity | | 52,180 |

Now, check to confirm assets = Liab. + Equity

Remember, the assets are the items an organization owns and uses to generate income. The L&E side is how the organization paid for those assets. Thus, the balance is between what one owns and how one paid for them. Keep this notion in mind when working with balance sheets.

## Income statement

An income statement covers a period of time and shows the activity, such as sales, expenses, and what the organization has left at the end of the period, known as net income. It is considered a means

**Surviving Introduction to Finance**

to assess how efficiently the organization uses its assets to produce net income. Think of it this way: In a simple company, Bobbie sells $200 of food and the food cost the company $150 to acquire materials and bake, then:

| | |
|---|---|
| Revenue | $200 |
| Cost of goods sold | $150 |
| Net income | $50 |

Now, if Bobbie moves operations out of her house, rents a store, and increases sales, operating expenses are added. Now, Bobbie sells $2,500 of food and the food cost the company $1,875 to acquire materials and bake, and $300 rent, then:

| | |
|---|---|
| Revenue | $2,500 |
| Cost of goods sold | $1,875 |
| Gross profit | $625 |
| Operating expense | $300 |
| Net income | $325 |

Just like the balance sheet, the income statement can become more involved over time and include more items, just like in this example:

| Ending period 12/2013 | | Amount |
|---|---|---|
| Revenue | | |
| Gross sales | | $30,000.00 |
| Less: Sales / returns | | $120.00 |
| Net Sales | | $29,880.00 |
| Cost of goods sold | | |
| Beginning inventory | $18,796.00 | |
| Add: purchases | $17,824.00 | |
| | $36,620.00 | |
| Less: ending inventory | $16,820.00 | |
| COGS | | $19,800.00 |
| Gross Profit (loss) | | $10,080.00 |
| Expenses: | | |
| Operating expenses | $4,000.00 | |
| Depreciation | $2,500.00 | |
| Total expenses before interest and taxes | | $6,500.00 |
| Earnings before Interest and taxes (EBIT) | | $3,580.00 |
| Interest expense | | $1,000.00 |
| Earnings before taxes (EBT) | | $2,580.00 |
| Taxes (35%) | | $903.00 |
| Net income (loss) - NI | | $1,677.00 |

The income statement follows an order beginning with sales, any adjustments to sales (such as discounts or returns), subtractions for costs of goods / services, then operating expenses. Earnings before interest and taxes (EBIT) is a common item one may focus on in finance as this is a reflection of net earnings available after operating activities; that is, what is left after costs associated with producing the sales. Earnings before taxes (EBT) is the earnings after any interest expense. This is a measure of what is left after operating expenses and explicit costs of financing them. Finally, Net Income (NI) is what is left after all expenses, including taxes, are subtracted.

Additional items on an income statement include Earnings per Share (EPS), which is found by net income divided by number of common shares outstanding. This is a measure of how much of each share's claim on net income. Dividends paid per share is money paid for each share held, a means to return cash to owners.  Dividend yield (dividend divided by stock price) is another measure of return for each share:

| | |
|---|---|
| Net income (loss) - NI | $1,677.00 |
| Shares outstanding | 1000 |
| Earnings per share (EPS) | $1.68 |
| Dividends paid, per share | $0.25 |
| Stock price 12/31/2013 | $  78.92 |
| Dividend yield | 0.32% |

Just like with the balance sheet, one may compare the income statement over time (horizontal analysis).  This analysis can show how net income has changed, for instance, falling 54.23%:

| Ending period 12/2013 | | Amount | Ending period 12/2012 | | Amount | Increase / decrease | % change |
|---|---|---|---|---|---|---|---|
| Revenue | | | Revenue | | | | |
| Gross sales | | $30,000.00 | Gross sales | | $28,500.00 | $ 1,500.00 | 5.26% |
| Less: Sales / returns | | $120.00 | Less: Sales / returns | | $140.00 | $ (20.00) | -14.29% |
| Net Sales | | $29,880.00 | Net Sales | | $28,360.00 | $ 1,520.00 | 5.36% |
| Cost of goods sold | | | Cost of goods sold | | | | |
| Beginning inventory | $18,796.00 | | Beginning inventory | $16,500.00 | | $ 2,296.00 | 13.92% |
| Add: purchases | $17,824.00 | | Add: purchases | $17,824.00 | | $ - | 0.00% |
| | $36,620.00 | | | $34,324.00 | | $ 2,296.00 | 6.69% |
| Less: ending inventory | $16,820.00 | | Less: ending inventory | $18,796.00 | | $ (1,976.00) | -10.51% |
| COGS | | $19,800.00 | COGS | | $15,528.00 | $ 4,272.00 | 27.51% |
| Gross Profit (loss) | | $10,080.00 | Gross Profit (loss) | | $12,832.00 | $ (2,752.00) | -21.45% |
| Expenses: | | | Expenses: | | | | |
| Operating expenses | $4,000.00 | | Operating expenses | $3,800.00 | | $ 200.00 | 5.26% |
| Depreciation | $2,500.00 | | Depreciation | $2,500.00 | | $ - | 0.00% |
| Total expenses before interest and taxes | | $6,500.00 | Total expenses before interest and taxes | | $6,300.00 | $ 200.00 | 3.17% |
| Earnings before interest and taxes (EBIT) | | $3,580.00 | Earnings before interest and taxes (EBIT) | | $6,532.00 | $ (2,952.00) | -45.19% |
| Interest expense | | $1,000.00 | Interest expense | | $895.00 | $ 105.00 | 11.73% |
| Earnings before taxes (EBT) | | $2,580.00 | Earnings before taxes (EBT) | | $5,637.00 | $ (3,057.00) | -54.23% |
| Taxes (35%) | | $903.00 | Taxes (35%) | | $1,972.95 | $ (1,069.95) | -54.23% |
| Net income (loss) - NI | | $1,677.00 | Net income (loss) - NI | | $3,664.05 | $ (1,987.05) | -54.23% |

How about an example of completing an income statement with the following information:

Net Sales are 47,181.50
Total operating expenses are 11,500
Cost of goods sold (COGS) are 16,760

Interest expense is 2,700
Taxes are 35%
What is net income?

Remember, sales are first, followed by cost of goods / services, then operating expenses to get to Earnings Before Interest and Taxes (EBIT), then interest expense to get to Earnings Before Taxes (EBT), then taxes, and finally Net Income (NI).

| | |
|---|---|
| Net Sales | 47,181.50 |
| Less COGS | 16,760 |
| Gross profit (loss)* | 30,421.50 |
| Less op. expenses | 11,500 |
| EBIT | 18,921.50 |
| Less interest exp. | 2,700 |
| EBT | 16,221.50 |
| Less taxes (35%) | 5,677.53 |
| Net Income (NI) | 10,543.98 |

* Note, losses are entered inside ( ).

Now, if there are 5,000 common shares outstanding, what is earnings per share (EPS)?

This is found NI / shares outstanding

So, EPS = 10,543.98 / 5,000 = $2.11

In sum, the order of the income statement is standardized. There may be more detail, but the order to get to NI and EPS is the same.

## Ratio analysis

Ratio analysis is helpful to see how an organization is doing over time (trend analysis) or compared to its peers in the industry. There are a large number of ratios one may calculate and they fall into five general categories: Liquidity, Operating efficiency (or activity),

**Surviving Introduction to Finance**

Leverage (or debt ratios), Profitability, and Market (or relative valuation).

Liquidity ratios are a means to measure how likely an organization will be able to pay its bills as they come due as well as how well it is using the current assets to produce revenue. These ratios include:

Current ratio (current assets / current liabilities);

Quick ratio ((current assets – inventory) / current liabilities);

Net working capital (current assets – current liabilities) - this one is not so much a ratio as a measure of capital available to assist with operations; and

Cash ratio ((cash + marketable securities) / current liabilities.

Operating efficiency (or activity) ratios are a means to measure how efficiently the organization is using assets, equity, inventory, receivables and the like to produce revenue. These ratios include:

Total asset turnover (sales / average total assets);

Equity turnover (sales / average equity);

Inventory turnover (COGS / average inventory);

Receivables turnover (net sales / average receivables); and

Average receivables collection period (365 / receivables turnover).

Debt or leverage ratios allow one to see how efficiently the organization is using debt to finance the asset side of the balance sheet. These ratios include:

Debt-to-assets ratio (total liabilities / total assets);

Debt-to-equity ratio (total liabilities / total equity); and

Interest coverage ratio (EBIT / interest expense).

Profitability ratios measure how well one utilizes the assets – and leverage – to produce various margins. These ratios include:

Gross margin on sales ((sales – cost of sales) / net sales;

Operating margin on sales (EBIT / net sales);

Net profit margin (net income / sales);

Return on equity (net income / equity); and

Return on total invested capital (ROIC): (net income + interest expense)/(interest bearing debt + equity).

Market – or relative valuation – ratios are a means to compare stock price and other data so comparisons can be made between multiple companies on a standardized basis. These are typically used when other metrics produce nonsense values or information is not available. These ratios include:

Price earnings ratio: (current market price / EPS);

Price to cash flow: (current market price / expected future cash flow per share); and

Price to sales: (current market price / expected sales per share).

Each ratio's strength depends on what one is measuring. A list of common ratios and strengths include:

# Surviving Introduction to Finance

| Financial Metrics | | |
|---|---|---|
| **Metric** | **Calculation** | **Strength** |
| Liquidity | | |
| Current ratio | current assets / current liabilities | Higher |
| Net working capital | current assets - current liabilities | Higher |
| Quick ratio | (current assets - inventories) / current liabilities | Higher |
| Cash ratio | cash / current liabilities | Higher |

| | | |
|---|---|---|
| Activity | | |
| Total asset turnover | sales / total assets | Higher |
| Fixed asset turnover | sales / fixed assets | Higher |
| Capital turnover | sales / (interest-bearing debt + equity) | Higher |
| Accounts receivable turnover | sales / accounts receivables | Higher |
| Accounts receivable days outstanding | 365 days / accounts receivable turnover | Lower |
| Inventory turnover | cost of goods sold / inventory | Higher |
| Inventory days outstanding | 365 days / inventory turnover | Lower |
| Accounts payable period | avg. AP / (COGS / 365) | Depends |

| | | |
|---|---|---|
| Leverage | | |
| Debt to equity | liabilities / equity | Lower |
| Financial leverage | assets / equity | Lower |
| Capitalization ratio | interest-bearing debt / (interest-bearing debt + equity) | Lower |
| Interest coverage | earnings before interest and tax / interest expense | Higher |
| Profitability | | |
| Net margin | net income / sales | Higher |
| Pretax margin | pretax income / sales | Higher |
| Operating margin | operating income / sales | Higher |
| Gross margin | (sales - cost of goods sold) / sales | Higher |
| Return on assets | net income / assets | Higher |
| Return on net assets | net income / (assets - non-interest-bearing curent liabilities) | Higher |
| Return on capital | EBIT (1 - tax rate) / (interest-bearing debt + equity) | Higher |
| Return on equity | net income / equity | Higher |

| Market | | | |
|---|---|---|---|
| Price / earnings ratio | Stock price per share / earnings per share | Higher |
| Market-to-book ratio | market value / book value | Higher |
| Shareholder returns | (capital appreciation + dividends) / beginning stock price | Higher |
| Dividend yield | dividends per share / beginning price | Higher |

Trend analysis involves comparing a company's ratios over time to see how they are changing. This can include using information from the balance sheet and income statements used in this presentation thus far along with the financial statements and ratio analysis worksheet provided. For example:

| Liquidity Ratios | Enter here | 2013 | Enter here | 2012 |
|---|---|---|---|---|
| **Current Ratio** | | | | |
| Current Assets | $ 23,580.00 | | $ 23,928.00 | |
| Current Liabilities | $ 2,129.00 | 11.08 | $ 2,812.00 | 8.51 |
| **Quick (Acid-Test) Ratio** | | | | |
| Current Assets-Inventory | $ 6,760.00 | | $ 5,132.00 | |
| Current Liabilities | $ 2,129.00 | 3.18 | $ 2,812.00 | 1.83 |
| **Inventory Turnover** | | | | |
| COGS | $ 17,606.00 | | $ 15,528.00 | |
| Average Inventory (beg. + end / 2) | $ 17,808.00 | 0.99 | $ 17,648.00 | 0.88 |
| **Avg. Inventory Processing Period** | | | | |
| 365 | | | | |
| Inventory Turnover | | 369.18778 | | 414.83256 |

Horizontal analysis involves computing ratios for a company at one point in time and then comparing these ratios to other companies in the industry at the same time as well. This analysis provides one with benchmark information about how well the organization may or may not be doing relative to others. The results can assist one with planning in the areas of operating efficiencies, capital structure (the L&E side of the balance sheet), as well as use of cash to pay bills as they come due.

Given the balance sheet and income statement on the following slides, find these ratios:

Current ratio

**Surviving Introduction to Finance**
Receivables Turnover
Average Receivables Collection Period
Payables Turnover
Payables Payment Period
Debt-to-asset ratio
Return on Equity
Price-Earnings Ratio

Using this balance sheet:

| Assets | Amount | 2013 | Percent |
|---|---|---|---|
| Current assets | | | |
| Cash | $ 4,500.00 | | 8.62% |
| Acc. Rec. | $ 6,200.00 | | 11.88% |
| Inventory | $ 21,980.00 | | 42.12% |
| Total current assets | $ 32,680.00 | | 62.63% |
| | | | |
| Plant and Equipment | | | |
| Equipment | $ 22,500.00 | | 43.12% |
| Accumulated Depreciation | $ (3,000.00) | | |
| Total P&E | $ 19,500.00 | | 37.37% |
| | | | |
| Total Asset | $ 52,180.00 | | 100.00% |
| | | | |
| Liabilities | | | |
| Current liabilities | | | |
| Acc. Payables | $ 11,500.00 | | 22.04% |
| Wages Payables | $ 1,400.00 | | 2.68% |
| Total current liabilities | $ 12,900.00 | | 24.72% |
| | | | |
| Long-term liabilities | | | |
| Note payable | $ 21,900.00 | | 41.97% |
| Total long-term liab. | $ 21,900.00 | | 41.97% |
| | | | |
| Total liabilities | $ 34,800.00 | | 66.69% |
| | | | |
| Owner's Equity | | | |
| Capital (equity) | $ 17,380.00 | | 33.31% |
| | | | |
| Total liabilities & Equity | $ 52,180.00 | | 100.00% |

and this income statement:

| Ending period 12/2013 | | Amount |
|---|---|---|
| Revenue | | |
| Gross sales | | $47,900.00 |
| Less: Sales / returns | | $718.50 |
| Net Sales | | $47,181.50 |
| Cost of goods sold | | |
| Beginning inventory | $22,900.00 | |
| Add: purchases | $15,840.00 | |
| | $38,740.00 | |
| Less: ending inventory | $21,980.00 | |
| COGS | | $16,760.00 |
| Gross Profit (loss) | | $30,421.50 |
| Expenses: | | |
| Operating expenses | $8,500.00 | |
| Depreciation | $3,000.00 | |
| Total expenses before interest and taxes | | $11,500.00 |
| Earnings before Interest and taxes (EBIT) | | $18,921.50 |
| Interest expense | | $2,700.00 |
| Earnings before taxes (EBT) | | $16,221.50 |
| Taxes (35%) | | $5,677.53 |
| Net income (loss) - NI | | $10,543.98 |
| Shares outstanding | | 5000 |
| Earnings per share (EPS) | | $2.11 |
| Dividends paid, per share | | $0.50 |
| Stock price 12/31/2013 | | $ 38.75 |
| Dividend yield | | 1.29% |

Current ratio = Current assets /Current liabilities

= 32,680 / 12,900 = 2.53

## Surviving Introduction to Finance

The values are located on the balance sheet, as indicated by the arrows.

| Assets | Amount | 2013 | Percent |
|---|---|---|---|
| Current assets | | | |
| Cash | $ 4,500.00 | | 8.62% |
| Acc. Rec. | $ 6,200.00 | | 11.88% |
| Inventory | $ 21,980.00 | | 42.12% |
| Total current assets | $ 32,680.00 | ← | 62.63% |
| | | | |
| Plant and Equipment | | | |
| Equipment | $ 22,500.00 | | 43.12% |
| Accumulated Depreciation | $ (3,000.00) | | |
| Total P&E | $ 19,500.00 | | 37.37% |
| | | | |
| Total Asset | $ 52,180.00 | | 100.00% |
| | | | |
| Liabilities | | | |
| Current liabilities | | | |
| Acc. Payables | $ 11,500.00 | | 22.04% |
| Wages Payables | $ 1,400.00 | | 2.68% |
| Total current liabilities | $ 12,900.00 | ← | 24.72% |
| | | | |
| Long-term liabilities | | | |
| Note payable | $ 21,900.00 | | 41.97% |
| Total long-term liab. | $ 21,900.00 | | 41.97% |
| | | | |
| Total liabilities | $ 34,800.00 | | 66.69% |
| | | | |
| Owner's Equity | | | |
| Capital (equity) | $ 17,380.00 | | 33.31% |
| | | | |
| Total liabilities & Equity | $ 52,180.00 | | 100.00% |

Receivables Turnover = net sales / average receivables

(if multiple periods are not present for average rec., just use what is on the balance sheet given.

Rec. Turnover = 47,181.50 / 6,200 = 7.61

This becomes an input, if requested, for the Average Receivables Collection Period, found by 365 / Rec. Turnover.

Using the 7.61 previously found, 365 / 7.61 = 47.96.
The information for both of these can be found in the statements below, as indicated by the arrows:

|  |  | 2013 |  |
|---|---|---|---|
| Assets | Amount |  | Percent |
| *Current assets* |  |  |  |
| Cash | $ 4,500.00 |  | 8.62% |
| Acc. Rec. | $ 6,200.00 | ⬅ | 11.88% |
| Inventory | $ 21,980.00 |  | 42.12% |
| *Total current assets* | $ 32,680.00 |  | 62.63% |

| Ending period 12/2013 |  |  | Amount |
|---|---|---|---|
| Revenue |  |  |  |
| Gross sales |  |  | $47,900.00 |
| Less: Sales / returns |  |  | $718.50 |
| Net Sales |  | ➡ | $47,181.50 |
| Cost of goods sold |  |  |  |

Payables Turnover = COGS / average acc. payables (if multiple periods are not present for average acc. payables, just use what is on the balance sheet given.

Payables Turnover = 16,760 / 11,500 = 1.46

The Payables Turnover is an input for the Payables Payment Period:

Payables payment period = 365 / payables turnover = 365 / 1.46 = 250

## Surviving Introduction to Finance

The information for both of these can be found in the statements below, as indicated by the arrows:

| Ending period 12/2013 | | Amount |
|---|---|---|
| Revenue | | |
| Gross sales | | $47,900.00 |
| Less: Sales / returns | | $718.50 |
| Net Sales | | $47,181.50 |
| Cost of goods sold | | |
| Beginning inventory | $22,900.00 | |
| Add: purchases | $15,840.00 | |
| | $38,740.00 | |
| Less: ending inventory | $21,980.00 | |
| COGS | ⟶ | $16,760.00 |

| Liabilities | | |
|---|---|---|
| *Current liabilities* | | |
| Acc. Payables | $ 11,500.00 ⟵ | 22.04% |
| Wages Payables | $ 1,400.00 | 2.68% |
| *Total current liabilities* | $ 12,900.00 | 24.72% |

Next is the Debt-to-asset ratio = Total liabilities / assets

= 34,800 / 52,180 = 0.67 or 67%

The information for this can be found in the balance sheet below, as indicated by the arrows:

| Assets | Amount | 2013 | Percent |
|---|---|---|---|
| Current assets | | | |
| Cash | $ 4,500.00 | | 8.62% |
| Acc. Rec. | $ 6,200.00 | | 11.88% |
| Inventory | $ 21,980.00 | | 42.12% |
| Total current assets | $ 32,680.00 | | 62.63% |
| | | | |
| Plant and Equipment | | | |
| Equipment | $ 22,500.00 | | 43.12% |
| Accumulated Depreciation | $ (3,000.00) | | |
| Total P&E | $ 19,500.00 | | 37.37% |
| | | | |
| Total Asset | $ 52,180.00 | ⟵ | 100.00% |
| | | | |
| Liabilities | | | |
| Current liabilities | | | |
| Acc. Payables | $ 11,500.00 | | 22.04% |
| Wages Payables | $ 1,400.00 | | 2.68% |
| Total current liabilities | $ 12,900.00 | | 24.72% |
| | | | |
| Long-term liabilities | | | |
| Note payable | $ 21,900.00 | | 41.97% |
| Total long-term liab. | $ 21,900.00 | | 41.97% |
| | | | |
| Total liabilities | $ 34,800.00 | ⟵ | 66.69% |
| | | | |
| Owner's Equity | | | |
| Capital (equity) | $ 17,380.00 | | 33.31% |
| | | | |
| Total liabilities & Equity | $ 52,180.00 | | 100.00% |

Return on equity = net income / equity

= 10,543.98 / 52,180  = 0.202 or 20.2%

The information for both of these can be found in the statements below, as indicated by the arrows:

## Surviving Introduction to Finance

| | | |
|---|---|---|
| Total expenses before interest and taxes | | $11,500.00 |
| Earnings before Interest and taxes (EBIT) | | $18,921.50 |
| Interest expense | | $2,700.00 |
| Earnings before taxes (EBT) | | $16,221.50 |
| Taxes (35%) | | $5,677.53 |
| Net income (loss) - NI | | $10,543.98 |

| Owner's Equity | | | |
|---|---|---|---|
| Capital (equity) | $ 17,380.00 | | 33.31% |
| | | | |
| Total liabilities & Equity | $ 52,180.00 | | 100.00% |

Price – earnings ratio = current market value of common stock / EPS

= 38.75 / 2.11 = 18.36

This is not a price; rather just a ratio. Essentially, this says the price is 18.36 times the earnings.

The information for this can be found in the income statement below, as indicated by the arrows:

| | | |
|---|---|---|
| Net income (loss) - NI | | $10,543.98 |
| Shares outstanding | | 5000 |
| Earnings per share (EPS) | | $2.11 |
| Dividends paid, per share | | $0.50 |
| Stock price 12/31/2013 | | $ 38.75 |
| Dividend yield | | 1.29% |

The following is the summary of above calculations:

Current ratio – 2.53
Receivables Turnover – 7.61
Average Receivables Collection Period – 47.96
Payables Turnover – 1.46

Payables Payment Period - 250
Debt-to-asset ratio – 67%
Return on Equity – 20.2%
Price-Earnings Ratio – 18.36

When working with ratios, keep in mind that sometimes what you are looking for has one input that is the result of another ratio. The list of common ratios covered in this chapter should help. Templates for common ratios may be found at my website:

www.askthatprofessor.com

# Surviving Introduction to Finance

# Chapter IV - Discounted Cash Flow analysis (DCF)

Discounted cash flow (DCF) analysis is a tool decision-makers use to determine if a project's cash flows are worth the investment. Future cash flows from the project that will occur if the project is accepted are discounted to the present using the PV lump sum formula covered in Chapter 2. The discount – or interest – rate used comes from a variety of sources, a topic likely covered in your finance course. The discounted future cash flows are then summed and the initial cash flow (the investment) is subtracted. Decision rules – covered later in this chapter – are used to make the decision.

## Net present value (NPV)

Let us start with an example using Net Present Value (NPV). You are considering an investment in Company A. This will require $100 up front and is expected to produce $10 in year 1, $60 in year 2 and $80 in year 3. Your best alternative investment is 10%. Should you invest in this project?

First step, list cash flows (CF) by year and the required rate of return. Excel, Calc, or Google's spreadsheet are great for DCF problems. Each cash flow (CF) is followed by the year (i.e CF0 is initial cash flow, CF1 is year 1 cash flow, etc), such as in this example:

|  | **Project A** |
|---|---|
| CF0 | $ (100.00) |
| CF1 | $ 10.00 |
| CF2 | $ 60.00 |
| CF3 | $ 80.00 |
|  |  |

The formula approach involves using the Present Value lump sum formula:

---

$$PV = FV / (1+r)^t$$

Discount each cash flow to the present by the number of years to the present:

$$10 / (1+0.10)^1 = \$9.09$$
$$60 / (1+0.10)^2 = \$49.59$$
$$80 / (1+0.10)^3 = \$60.11$$

Note the exponent changes for each year the cash flow occurs (i.e. 10 occurs in year 1 so its exponent is 1, 60 occurs in year 2 so its exponent is 2 and 80 in year 3 so it uses an exponent of 3).

Sum the three cash flows to get \$118.78. This is the value of the future cash flows today. To find out what the net present value (NPV) of this investment is, subtract the initial \$100 investment. This gives you the \$18.78. \$18.78 is how much you can expect to make above your investment factoring in the return of 10% you could get elsewhere.

Excel, Calc, and Google spreadsheet has a function NPV that can be used here:

=npv(rate,value1... value n)-initial cash flow

Rate is the appropriate discount rate, in this case, 10% or 0.10 (remember, enter percentages in decimal equivalent form).

=npv(0.10,10,60,80)-100

A typical set up looks like this:

|  | Project A |
|---|---|
| CF0 | $ (100.00) |
| CF1 | $ 10.00 |
| CF2 | $ 60.00 |
| CF3 | $ 80.00 |
|  |  |
| Rate of ret. | 10.00% |
| NPV | $18.78 |

## Internal rate of return (IRR)

Another approach to valuing a project like this is to find the rate of return the future cash flows will provide for the initial investment. This process is known as Internal Rate of Return (IRR). Essentially, IRR is a compound time value of money problem where one solves for the rate that makes all future cash flow's present value equal the initial investment, or $0, when the initial cash flow is subtracted from the sum of present value of future cash flows.

If all future cash flows are exactly the same, one could simply use the present value of an annuity formula covered in Chapter 2. However, since this formula requires that all cash flows be exactly the same, it cannot be used for projects like Company A. Fortunately, the math of IRR can be easily handled by Excel, Calc, and Google spreadsheets using the =IRR(values) function. Using the same information from the set-up in the spreadsheet, just go to an empty cell, type in =IRR(range) except where range is, highlight all cash flows. It is important to note here the initial cash flow has to be entered as a negative value or there will be an error returned. I have these cash flows set up in columns A and B beginning at row 1:

## Surviving Introduction to Finance

|  | Project A |
|---|---|
| CF0 | $ (100.00) |
| CF1 | $ 10.00 |
| CF2 | $ 60.00 |
| CF3 | $ 80.00 |
|  |  |
| Rate of ret. | 10.00% |
| NPV | $18.78 |
| IRR | 18.13% |

Function is:  =IRR(B2:B5) where B2:B5 is the highlighted column that includes -100, 10, 60, and 80, to get 18.13%. 18.13% is the rate that is used in NPV to discount each cash flow would result in a NPV of $0.

## Payback method

Another – and much simpler – DCF is the payback method. This approach looks for the amount of time it will take to breakeven at $0. One begins with the initial cash outflow as a negative number and then adds each new cash flow until $0 is reached. Begin with year 0, add $10 to get -$90, another $60 gives -$30. The third year will more than get one to $0 so a partial year calculation is used. $30 / $80 = 0.375. Add this 0.375 partial year to the two full years to get a payback of 2.375 years.

| Payback period | Cash flow | Balance |
|---|---|---|
| Year 0 | $ (100.00) | $ (100.00) |
| Year 1 | $ 10.00 | $ (90.00) |
| Year 2 | $ 60.00 | $ (30.00) |
| Year 3 | $ 80.00 | $ - |
| partial year calculation: |  | 0.375 |
| Payback time: |  | 2.375 |

# Decision rules

When NPV is at or above $0, accept the project; otherwise reject. When IRR is equal to or greater than the required return, accept the project; otherwise reject. For payback, accept whenever the payback is equal to or less than desired payback period.

When choosing between mutually exclusive projects – one can only accept one or a limited number of projects, one may rank the projects by NPV, IRR or payback results. The project with the highest NPV or IRR (or lowest payback) should be chosen.

You can also rank by Profitability Index (PI) by taking the sum of present value cash flows and dividing by initial investment. So, for Company A, PI = 118.78 / 100 = 1.19.

Now, consider the previously covered Company A with a second project Company B. Using the same approaches, consider whether B would be accepted along with A and, if mutually exclusive, which would be selected. Accept both; or if mutually exclusive, choose B:

| | Project A | Formula approach | | Probject B | Formula approach |
|---|---|---|---|---|---|
| CF0 | $ (100.00) | $ (100.00) | | $(100.00) | $ (100.00) |
| CF1 | $ 10.00 | $ 9.09 | | $ 70.00 | $ 63.64 |
| CF2 | $ 60.00 | $ 49.59 | | $ 50.00 | $ 41.32 |
| CF3 | $ 80.00 | $ 60.11 | | $ 20.00 | $ 15.03 |
| | | $ 18.78 | Sum | | $ 19.98 |
| Rate of ret. | 10.00% | | | 10.00% | |
| NPV | $18.78 | | | $19.98 | |
| IRR | 18.13% | | | 23.56% | |
| | | | | | |
| PI | 1.19 | | | 1.20 | |
| Payback period | Cash flow | Balance | | Cash flow | Balance |
| Year 0 | $ (100.00) | $ (100.00) | | $(100.00) | $ (100.00) |
| Year 1 | $ 10.00 | $ (90.00) | | $ 70.00 | $ (30.00) |
| Year 2 | $ 60.00 | $ (30.00) | | $ 50.00 | $ - |
| Year 3 | $ 80.00 | $ - | | $ 20.00 | NA |
| partial year calculation: | | 0.375 | partial year calculation: | | 0.600 |
| Payback time: | | 2.375 | Payback time: | | 1.600 |
| Decision? | | | Decision? | | |
| NPV | Accept | | NPV | Accept | |
| IRR | Accept | | IRR | Accept | |
| Mutually exclusive decision: | | | | | |
| NPV rule | Choose B | | | | |
| IRR rule | Choose B | | | | |

So, in sum, Company A has the following:

NPV = $18.78
IRR = 18.13%
Payback = 2.375 years
PI = 1.19

Company B has the following:

NPV = $19.98
IRR = 23.56%
Payback = 1.60
PI = 1.20

When working with discounted cash flow analyses, a spreadsheet is quite valuable as a means to organize and perform calculations in one area. It also allows one to copy / paste results into documents, such as reports, or presentation software. Templates for common ratios may be found at my website:

www.askthatprofessor.com

## Chapter V - Securities / industry analysis

We examine the three most common securities an introduction to finance student will work with in this chapter: 1) preferred stock, 2) common stock, and 3) bonds. The most common formulas are discussed, including the Dividend Discount Model (DDM) and Capital Asset Pricing Model (CAPM). Bond pricing was introduced in Chapter 2 and will be reviewed here.

### Preferred stock

Preferred stock is a hybrid security that typically has a common stock (equity) aspect and a fixed income aspect, like a bond. Of course, like many securities, there are a variety of these in structure but for purposes of this module, the focus is on a typical preferred stock, one with a stated dividend. The typical preferred stock formula is:

$$P0 = D / r$$

where P0 is the price of the stock today, D is the dividend and r is the required return. For example, a preferred stock with a 5% dividend on a $50 par stock would pay 5% of $50, or $2.50 per share held. At first issue, the formula, P0=D / r, holds true.

$$P0 = 2.50 / 0.05 = \$50.$$

Now, if you want to sell this security to someone and his or required return for this type of security is 7%, he or she would be willing to pay:

$$P0 = 2.50 / 0.07$$

Here, use 7% for r as this is how the potential buyer will value the cash flow of $2.50. P0 = $35.71.

One could also solve for the other variables if two of them are provided. For example, if this same preferred stock is now selling for $40, what is the implied required return? Using algebraic manipulation from Chapter 1, P0 = D / r, and by rearranging, one has:

$$r = D / P0$$

So, r = 2.50 / 40 or r = 0.0625 or 6.25%.

# Common stock

One of the most common stock formulas in finance is the Dividend Discount Model (DDM), constant growth:

$$P_0 = D_1 /(r-g)$$

This says the price today of a stock is equal to the expected dividend (D1) one period from now divided by the difference of the required return (the variable r) and the growth rate (g). You may note that if the growth rate is expected to be 0%, the g drops out leaving one with the preferred stock pricing formula P0 = D / r.

An example will illustrate. What is the price of a stock that is expected to pay a dividend of $2.00, has a required return of 12%, and a growth rate of 6%? (note, enter % values as decimal equivalents, as previously noted in Chapter 2).

$$P_0 = D_1 /(r-g)$$

$$P_0 = 2/(0.12 - 0.06)$$
$$P_0 = 2/0.06 = \$33.33$$

Sometimes one is given a dividend that is just paid. Since DDM uses the expected dividend one period from now, the current dividend must be adjusted to reflect the expected dividend. This can be done by:

$$D_1 = D_0(1+g)$$

Then, place the result of this into the DDM formula. Consider a stock that has recently paid a dividend of $0.75, has an expected growth rate of 8%, and a required return of 10%. What is the expected price?

$$D_1 = 0.75(1 + 0.10)$$
$$D_1 = 0.83$$
$$P_0 = 0.83/(0.10 - 0.08)$$
$$P_0 = \$41.50$$

There are other variations of this formula where one is asked to find other variables given all but one of the inputs. For example, if you are asked to find the required return for a stock given the dividend, price and growth rate, the rearranged formula is:

$$r = (D_1/P_0) + g$$

So, if you have a stock that is priced at $35, an expected growth rate of 5%, and an expected dividend of $0.90, the required return is:

$$r = (0.90/35) + 0.05$$
$$r = 0.026 + 0.05$$
$$r = 0.076 \rightarrow 7.6\%$$

Another variation asks you to find the growth rate given the other inputs. For example, if you are asked to find the expected growth rate for a stock given the dividend, price and required return, the rearranged formula is:

$$g = r - (D_1 / P_0)$$

So, if you have a stock that is priced at $28, a required return of 9%, and an expected dividend of $0.45, the expected growth rate is:

$$g = 0.09 - (0.45 / 28)$$
$$g = 0.09 - 0.016$$
$$g = 0.074 \rightarrow 7.4\%$$

Another frequently encountered common stock formula is the Capital Asset Pricing Model (CAPM), which includes the previously mentioned beta, $\beta$:

$$E(r) = R_{RF} + \beta(R_M - R_{RF})$$

This formula provides one with an expected return of a given stock based on how it varies with an index, such as the S&P500, Russell 2000, or Wilshire 5000 as well as the risk-free rate. Inputs are:

$$R_{RF}$$
$$R_M$$
$$\beta$$

and are the risk-free rate, return on market, and beta, in that order. Here is an example to illustrate. A company's beta is 1.25, the return on the S&P500 is 9.5% and the current risk-free rate on a US Treasury is 3%, what is the expected return of this stock?

$$E(r) = 0.03 + 1.25(0.095 - 0.03)$$
$$E(r) = 0.03 + 1.25(0.065)$$
$$E(r) = 0.03 + 0.08125$$
$$E(r) = 0.1113 \_ or \_ 11.13\%$$

One may also be given the expected return, risk-free rate, and market return and asked to find the beta. For example, a stock has an expected return of 14%, a risk-free rate of 2.5%, and a market return of 11%. What is the beta?

$$0.14 = 0.025 + \beta(0.11 - 0.025)$$
$$0.14 = 0.025 + \beta(0.085)$$
$$0.14 - 0.025 = 0.025 - 0.025 + \beta(0.085)$$
$$0.115 = \beta(0.085)$$
$$0.115 / 0.085 = [\beta(0.085)] / 0.085$$
$$1.35 = \beta$$

# Bonds

A bond is a compound time value of money problem as the typical bond contains a lump sum (par value returned at maturity) and a series of periodic payments. After a bond has been issued and begins trading in the secondary market, the market rates are used to price the bond while the stated coupon rate on the bond is used to determine the periodic payments. Excel is the ideal utility for bond valuation problems as one may find rate (also known as yield to maturity) and current price, among others, when given key information.

Now, consider a bond with a stated coupon rate of 7% and 9 years left to maturity. New bonds of this risk level are currently paying 6%. What is current price? Use Excel's =PV function:

=PV(RATE,NPER,PMT,FV,TYPE)

**Surviving Introduction to Finance**

RATE is the current market rate of 6%, or 0.06; NPER is 9; PMT is the coupon rate times par, or 7% * 1000 = 70; FV is the par value of 1000 (assumed to be 1000 unless otherwise informed), and type is 0.

=PV(0.06,9,70,1000,0) = $1,068.02

This bond is selling at a premium to par as its stated coupon rate is higher than what the new ones of comparable risk are selling for in the current market.

One may also find the yield to maturity (YTM) of a bond selling in the secondary market given the market price of the bond, the stated coupon rate, and time to maturity. A typical par value of a bond is $1,000 unless otherwise stated. For example, a bond selling for $1,145 with 8 years to maturity and a stated coupon rate of 6% has a YTM of:

Inputs are: PV = -1,145; NPER = 8; PMT = 0.06*1000 = 60; FV=1,000

=RATE(NPER,PMT,PV,FV)

=RATE(8,60,-1145,1000) = 0.0386 or 3.86%

Templates for securities analysis may be found at my website:

www.askthatprofessor.com

# About the Author

James M. Triplett is a Full-time Staff Faculty at University of Phoenix. He has taught corporate finance and securities analysis at the undergraduate and graduate levels since 2004 and is a former Chief Financial Officer, economist and ethicist with experience in the private and government sectors. He received his Bachelor of Arts in Management (Finance and Human Resource Management) from Mercyhurst College, a Master of Business Administration (Finance) from Gannon University, a Master of Science in Organizational Leadership from Mercyhurst College, an ABD toward a PhD in Organization and Management (Leadership) at Capella University where he worked on Organizational Design and Al-Qaeda ( A Case Study of the Structure of a Fundamentalist Islamic Terror Network), and is currently finishing a Master of Arts in Instructional Design Technology at West Virginia University. Jim is the 2009 University of Phoenix Midwest Region Gold recipient for Advancement of Scholarly Activity for his publications and 2009 Outstanding Faculty UBAM (Undergraduate Business Administration) Cleveland campus.